PIANO • VOCAL • GUITAR

ULTIMATE

BROADWAY

GOLD

100

◆ 100 OF THE BEST ◆

D1249758

ISBN 0-88188-155-4

A Joint Publication of
MPL COMMUNICATIONS, INC.
and
HAL•LEONARD
CORPORATION
7777 W. BLUEMOUND RD. P.O. BOX 13819 MILWAUKEE, WI 53213

PIANO • VOCAL • GUITAR
ULTIMATE
BROADWAY
GOLD

Contents Alphabetical by Show

Contents Alphabetical by Song Title

CIVILIZATION
(BONGO, BONGO, BONGO)
from the Broadway Musical ANGEL IN THE WINGS

Words and Music by BOB HILLIARD
and CARL SIGMAN

TOMORROW
from the Musical Production ANNIE

Lyric by MARTIN CHARNIN
Music by CHARLES STROUSE

The sun-'ll come out _____ to-mor-row,
bet your bot-tom dol-lar that to-mor-row _____ there'll be
sun! Jus' think-ing a-bout _____ to-mor-row

9

EASY STREET
from the Musical Production ANNIE

Lyric by MARTIN CHARNIN
Music by CHARLES STROUSE

BEAUTY AND THE BEAST
from Walt Disney's BEAUTY AND THE BEAST

Lyrics by HOWARD ASHMAN
Music by ALAN MENKEN

17

19

ANYTHING YOU CAN DO
from the Stage Production ANNIE GET YOUR GUN

Words and Music by
IRVING BERLIN

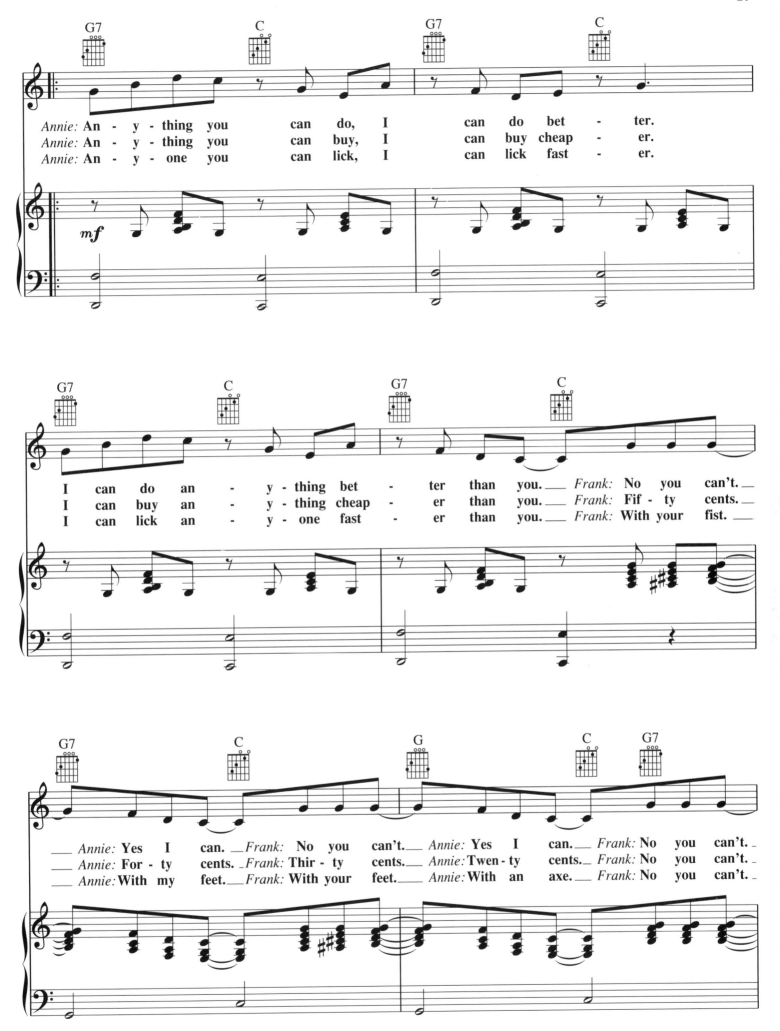

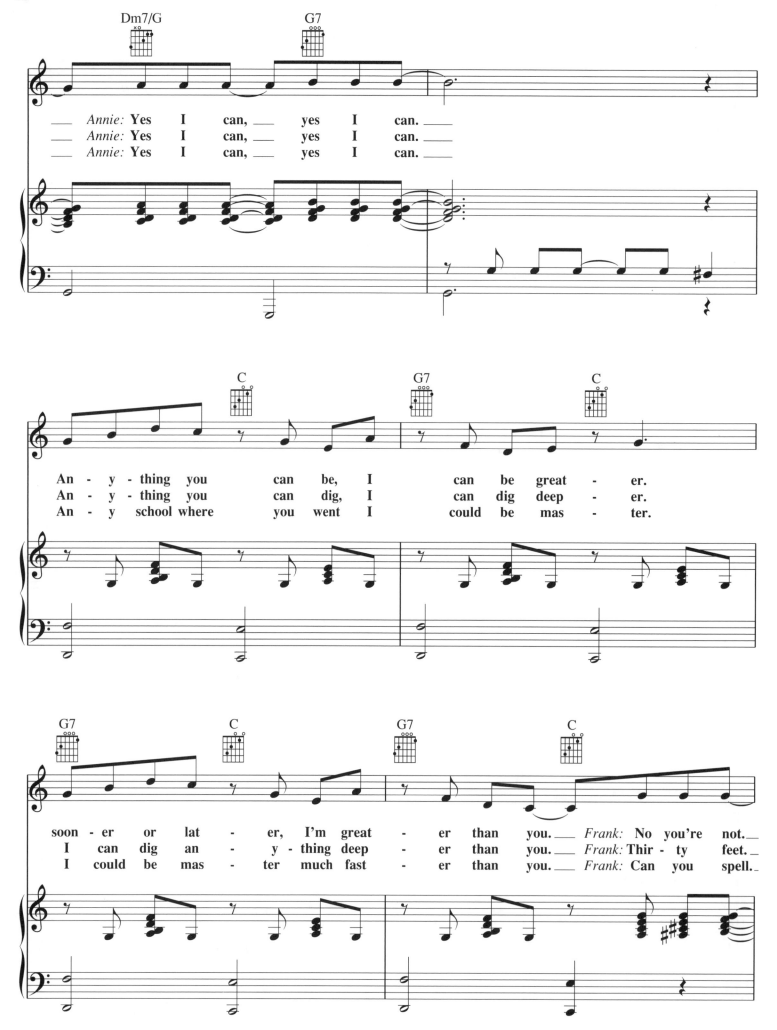

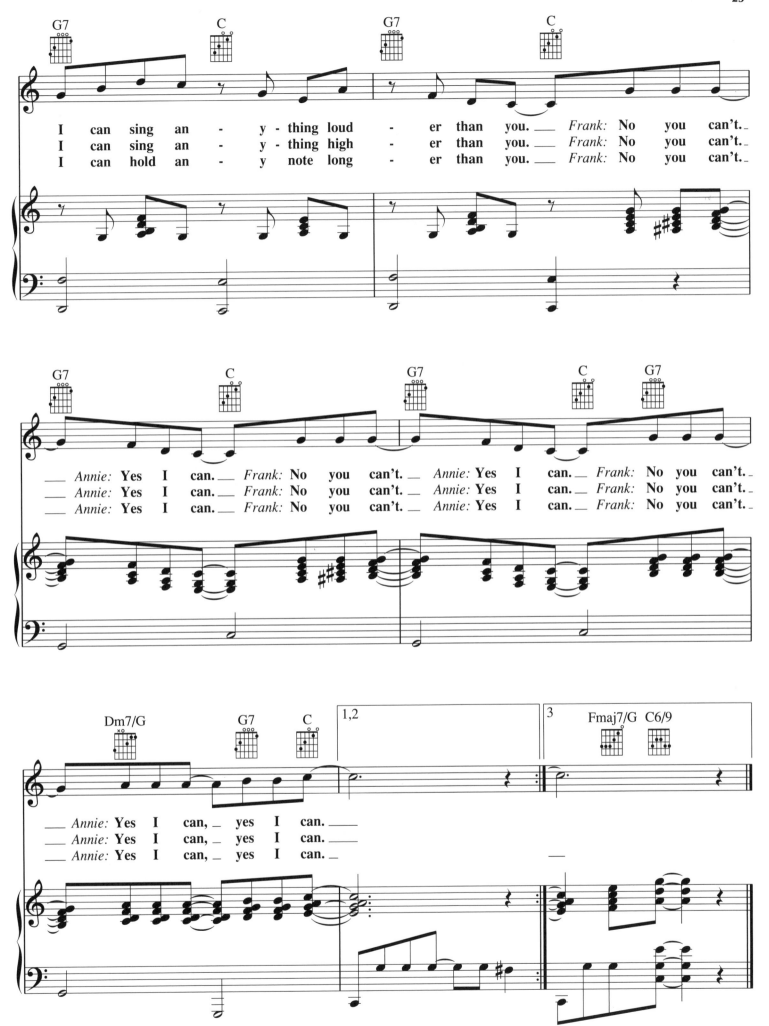

THEY SAY IT'S WONDERFUL

from the Stage Production ANNIE GET YOUR GUN

Words and Music by
IRVING BERLIN

HEAT WAVE
from the Stage Production AS THOUSANDS CHEER

Words and Music by
IRVING BERLIN

33

way that she moves ___ that ther-mo-me-ter proves ___ that she

cer-tain-ly can ___ can can. We're can can.

can - can. It's so hot the weath-er man will tell you

a re-cord's been made. ___

LOVE CHANGES EVERYTHING
from ASPECTS OF LOVE

Music by ANDREW LLOYD WEBBER
Lyrics by DON BLACK and CHARLES HART

Off _____ in- to the world we go, plan- ning fu- tures, shap- ing years.

Love _____ bursts in and sud- den- ly, all our wis- dom dis- ap- pears.

Love _____ makes fools of ev- ery- one: all the rules we make are

THE LADY IS A TRAMP
from BABES IN ARMS

Words by LORENZ HART
Music by RICHARD RODGERS

MY FUNNY VALENTINE
from BABES IN ARMS

Words by LORENZ HART
Music by RICHARD RODGERS

I'm a funny Valentine

A Comic Valentine

I'll make you smile from your heart

My looks are laughable

Unphotographable

I'm definitely not a work of art

My figure's less than Greek

My mouth's a little weak

When I open it to speak

I'm not smart

I can't change a thing for you

Even if I wanted to

This is the way it has to stay

Cause My birthday's Valentines Day

LONG BEFORE I KNEW YOU
from BELLS ARE RINGING

Words by BETTY COMDEN and ADOLPH GREEN
Music by JULE STYNE

BLUE SKIES
from BETSY

Words and Music by
IRVING BERLIN

52

(I WONDER WHY?)
YOU'RE JUST IN LOVE
from the Stage Production CALL ME MADAM

Words and Music by
IRVING BERLIN

I hear sing-ing and there's no one there.

I smell blos-soms and the trees are bare.

All day long I seem to walk on air, I won-der

IT'S A LOVELY DAY TODAY

from the Stage Production CALL ME MADAM

Words and Music by
IRVING BERLIN

IT'S ALL RIGHT WITH ME

from CAN-CAN

Words and Music by
COLE PORTER

Steadily moving fox trot

It's the wrong time _____ and the wrong place _____ tho' your face is charm-

-ing it's the wrong face, _____ it's not {her}{his} face _____ but such a charm-ing face

_____ that It's All Right _____ With Me. _____ It's the wrong song _____

C'EST MAGNIFIQUE
from CAN-CAN

Words and Music by
COLE PORTER

Moderately

When love comes in and takes you for a spin, oo la la-la,____ *C'est Mag - ni - fi - que. When ev - 'ry night your loved one holds you tight, oo la la-la,____

*Pronounced "say man-yee-fee-kuh"

I LOVE PARIS

from CAN-CAN

Words and Music by
COLE PORTER

JUNE IS BUSTIN' OUT ALL OVER
from CAROUSEL

Lyrics by OSCAR HAMMERSTEIN II
Music by RICHARD RODGERS

June is bust-in' out all o - ver! _____ All
June is bust-in' out all o - ver! _____ The

o - ver the mead-ow and the hill! _____ Buds 're
feel - in' is get - tin' so in - tense, _____ that the

bust-in' out a bush-es and the romp-in' riv-er push-es ev-'ry
young Vir-gin-ia creep-ers have been hug-gin' the be - jeep-ers out a

MEMORY
from CATS

Music by ANDREW LLOYD WEBBER
Text by TREVOR NUNN after T.S. ELIOT

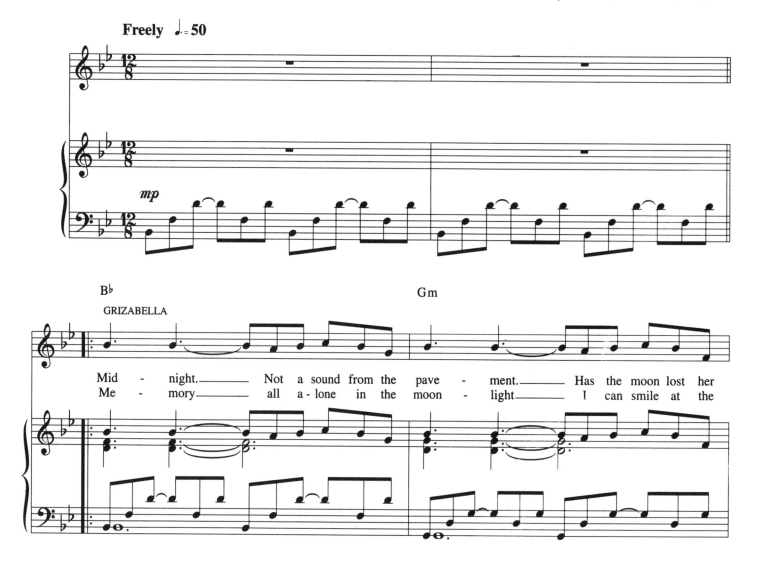

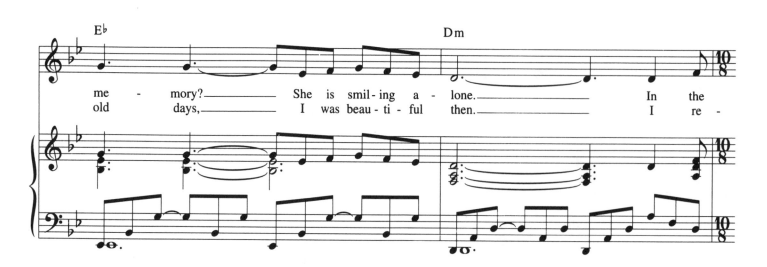

GRIZABELLA

Mid - night._____ Not a sound from the pave - ment._____ Has the moon lost her
Me - mory_____ all a - lone in the moon - light_____ I can smile at the

me - mory?_____ She is smil - ing a - lone._____ In the
old days,_____ I was beau - ti - ful then._____ I re -

ONE
from A CHORUS LINE

Music by MARVIN HAMLISCH
Lyric by EDWARD KLEBAN

WHAT I DID FOR LOVE
from A CHORUS LINE

Music by MARVIN HAMLISCH
Lyric by EDWARD KLEBAN

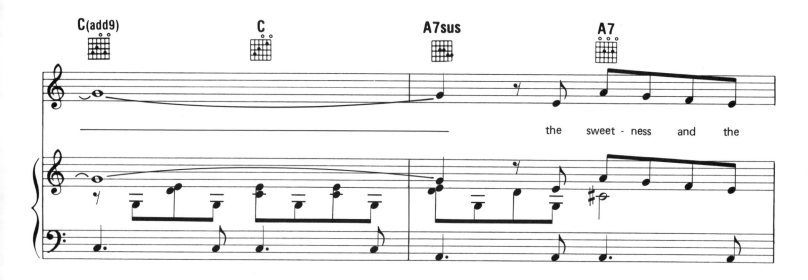

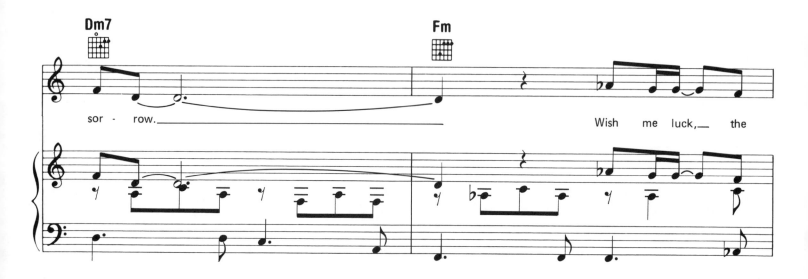

THE BEST IN THE WORLD
from A DAY IN HOLLYWOOD

Music and Lyric by
JERRY HERMAN

I DON'T WANT TO KNOW
from DEAR WORLD

Music and Lyric by
JERRY HERMAN

DO I HEAR A WALTZ?

from DO I HEAR A WALTZ?

Music by RICHARD RODGERS
Lyrics by STEPHEN SONDHEIM

99

MAKE SOMEONE HAPPY
from DO RE MI

Words by BETTY COMDEN and ADOLPH GREEN
Music by JULE STYNE

SHE (HE) TOUCHED ME
from DRAT! THE CAT!

Lyric by IRA LEVIN
Music by MILTON SCHAFER

SOON IT'S GONNA RAIN
from THE FANTASTICKS

Words by TOM JONES
Music by HARVEY SCHMIDT

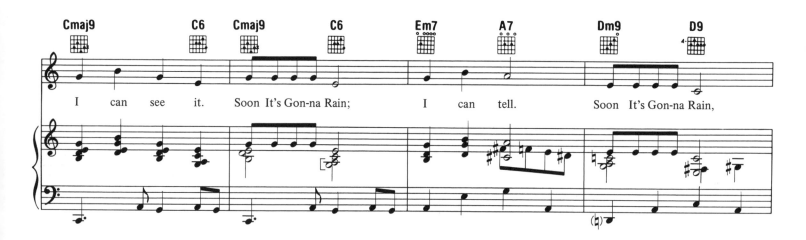

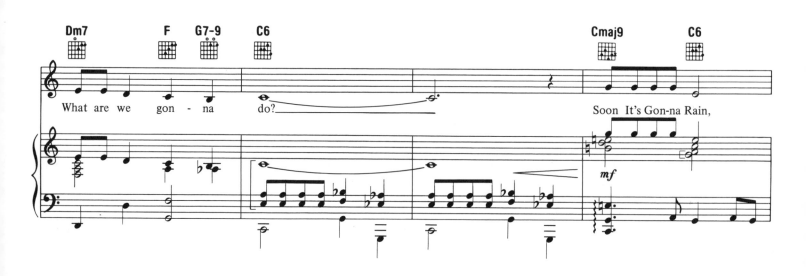

LOVE, LOOK AWAY
from FLOWER DRUM SONG

Lyrics by OSCAR HAMMERSTEIN II
Music by RICHARD RODGERS

OLD DEVIL MOON

from FINIAN'S RAINBOW

Words by E.Y. HARBURG
Music by BURTON LANE

YOU ARE WOMAN, I AM MAN
from FUNNY GIRL

Words by BOB MERRILL
Music by JULE STYNE

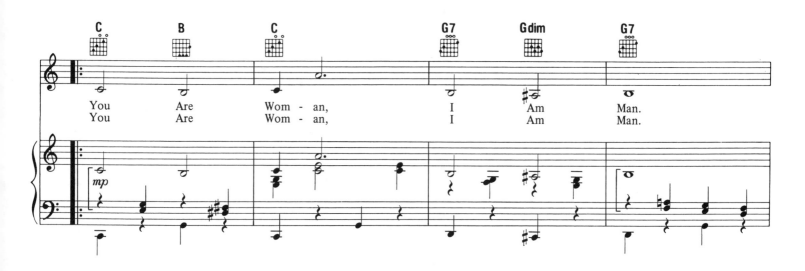

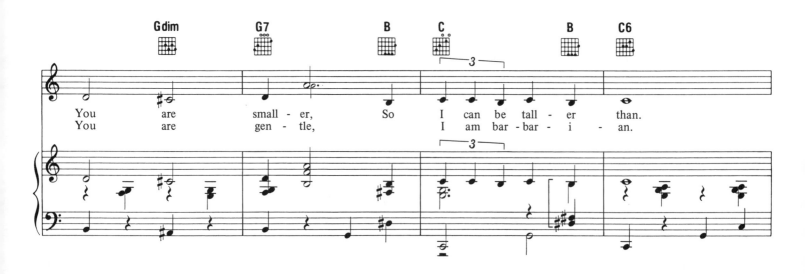

COMEDY TONIGHT
from A FUNNY THING HAPPENED ON THE WAY TO THE FORUM

Words and Music by
STEPHEN SONDHEIM

Brightly

Lyrics:

Some-thing fa-mil - iar, some-thing pe - cul - iar,
Some-thing con-vul - sive, some-thing re - pul - sive,

Some-thing for ev - 'ry-one, a Com-e-dy To - night!
Some-thing for ev - 'ry-one, a Com-e-dy To - night!

Some-thing ap - peal - ing, some-thing ap - pal - ling,
Some-thing es - thet - ic, some-thing fre - net - ic,

THE VARSITY DRAG

from GOOD NEWS

Words and Music by B.G. DESYLVA,
LEW BROWN and RAY HENDERSON

SUMMER NIGHTS
from GREASE

Lyric and Music by WARREN CASEY
and JIM JACOBS

Moderately

Boy: "Sum-mer lov-in', had me a blast."
"She swam by me; she got a cramp."
"Took her bowl-ing in the ar-cade."

Girl: "Sum-mer lov-in' hap-pened so fast."
"He ran by me; got my suit damp."
"We went stroll-ing; drank lem-on-ade."

Boy: "Met a girl, cra-zy for me."
"Saved her life; she near-ly drowned."
"We made out un-der the dock."

Girl: "Met a boy, cute as can be."
"He showed off, splash-ing a-round."
"We stayed out till ten o-clock."

Sum-mer days drift-ing a-way to, uh, oh, those Sum-mer Nights. Well-a, well-a, well-a
Sum-mer sun, some-thing's be-gun. But, uh, oh, those Sum-mer Nights.
Sum-mer fling don't mean a thing. But,

Tacet

A BUSHEL AND A PECK
from GUYS AND DOLLS

By FRANK LOESSER

Light Bounce Tempo

I love you   A Bu - shel And   A Peck   A Bu - shel And   A Peck   and a
I love you   A Bu - shel And   A Peck   A Bu - shel And   A Peck   tho' you
I love you   A Bu - shel And   A Peck   A Bu - shel And   A Peck   and it

hug   a - round   the neck   Hug   a - round   the neck   and a   bar - rel   and   a heap
make   my heart   a wreck   Make   my heart   a wreck   and you   make my   life   a mess
beats   me all   to heck   Beats   me all   to heck   how I'll   ev - er   tend   the farm

Bar - rel and   a heap   and I'm   talk - in' in   my sleep   a - bout   you
Make   my life   a mess   yes   a   mess of hap - pi - ness   a - bout
Ev - er   tend   the farm   when I   wan - na keep   my arm   a - bout

GUYS AND DOLLS
from GUYS AND DOLLS

By FRANK LOESSER

I'LL KNOW
from GUYS AND DOLLS

By FRANK LOESSER

I'VE NEVER BEEN IN LOVE BEFORE
from GUYS AND DOLLS

By FRANK LOESSER

IF I WERE A BELL
from GUYS AND DOLLS

By FRANK LOESSER

Medium Bounce

Ask me how do I feel___ Ask me now that we're co-sy and cling - ing___
how do I feel___ From this Chem-is-try les-son I'm learn - ing___

Well sir, all I can say___ is if I___ were a bell___ I'd be
Well sir, all I can say___ is if I___ were a bridge___ I'd be

ring - ing.___ From the mo-ment we kissed to - nite___
burn - ing.___ Yes, I knew my mor - ale would crack___

LUCK BE A LADY
from GUYS AND DOLLS

By FRANK LOESSER

LET ME ENTERTAIN YOU

from GYPSY

Words by STEPHEN SONDHEIM
Music by JULE STYNE

So let me en-ter-tain you, Let me make you smile. Let me do a few tricks, some old and then some new tricks, I'm ver-y ver-sa-tile. And if you're real good,

BEFORE THE PARADE PASSES BY

from HELLO, DOLLY!

Music and Lyric
by JERRY HERMAN

HELLO, DOLLY!

from HELLO, DOLLY!

Music and Lyric by
JERRY HERMAN

IT ONLY TAKES A MOMENT
from HELLO, DOLLY!

Music and Lyric by
JERRY HERMAN

152

PINE CONES AND HOLLY BERRIES

from HERE'S LOVE

Words and Music by
MEREDITH WILLSON

I STILL GET JEALOUS

from the Broadway Musical HIGH BUTTON SHOES

Lyric by SAMMY CAHN
Music by JULE STYNE

A SLEEPIN' BEE
from HOUSE OF FLOWERS

Lyric by TRUMAN CAPOTE and HAROLD ARLEN
Music by HAROLD ARLEN

YOU'RE THE CREAM IN MY COFFEE
from HOLD EVERYTHING

Words and Music by B.G. DeSYLVA,
LEW BROWN and RAY HENDERSON

BROTHERHOOD OF MAN
from HOW TO SUCCEED IN BUSINESS WITHOUT REALLY TRYING

By FRANK LOESSER

I BELIEVE IN YOU
from HOW TO SUCCEED IN BUSINESS WITHOUT REALLY TRYING

By FRANK LOESSER

PUSH DE BUTTON
from JAMAICA

Lyric by E.Y. HARBURG
Music by HAROLD ARLEN

Calypso Moderately Bright

All you do is Push De But - ton. up de el - e - va - tor.
Push De But - ton. up de hel - e - cop - ter.

Push De But - ton out de or - ange juice. Push De But - ton
Push De But - ton click de tel - e - phone. Push De But - ton

from re - frig - er - a - tor come ba - na - na short cake and fro - zen goose.
from de tel - e - vis - ion come de Pep - to Bis - mo with bar - i - tone.

Push De But - ton wipe de win - dow wip - er. Push De But - ton
Push De But - ton out come Pag - li - ac - ci. Push De But - ton

OUR LANGUAGE OF LOVE

from IRMA LA DOUCE

Music by MARGUERITE MONNOT
Original French words by ALEXANDRE BREFFORT
English words by JULIAN MORE,
DAVID HENEKER and MONTY NORMAN

SHALL WE DANCE?
from THE KING AND I

Lyrics by OSCAR HAMMERSTEIN II
Music by RICHARD RODGERS

I WHISTLE A HAPPY TUNE
from THE KING AND I

Lyrics by OSCAR HAMMERSTEIN II
Music by RICHARD RODGERS

I AM WHAT I AM

from LA CAGE AUX FOLLES

Music and Lyric by
JERRY HERMAN

BRING HIM HOME

from LES MISÉRABLES

Music by CLAUDE-MICHEL SCHÖNBERG
Lyrics by HERBERT KRETZMER and ALAIN BOUBLIL

LOST IN THE STARS
from the Musical Production LOST IN THE STARS

Words by MAXWELL ANDERSON
Music by KURT WEILL

Moderato assai

I WON'T SEND ROSES

from MACK AND MABEL

Music and Lyric by
JERRY HERMAN

Moderately

mf

I won't send ros - es, or hold the door;
fran - tic, my tem - per's cross;

I won't re - mem - ber which dress you wore.
With words ro - man - tic I'm at a loss.

My heart is too much in con - trol, the lack of
I'd be the first one to a - gree that I'm pre -

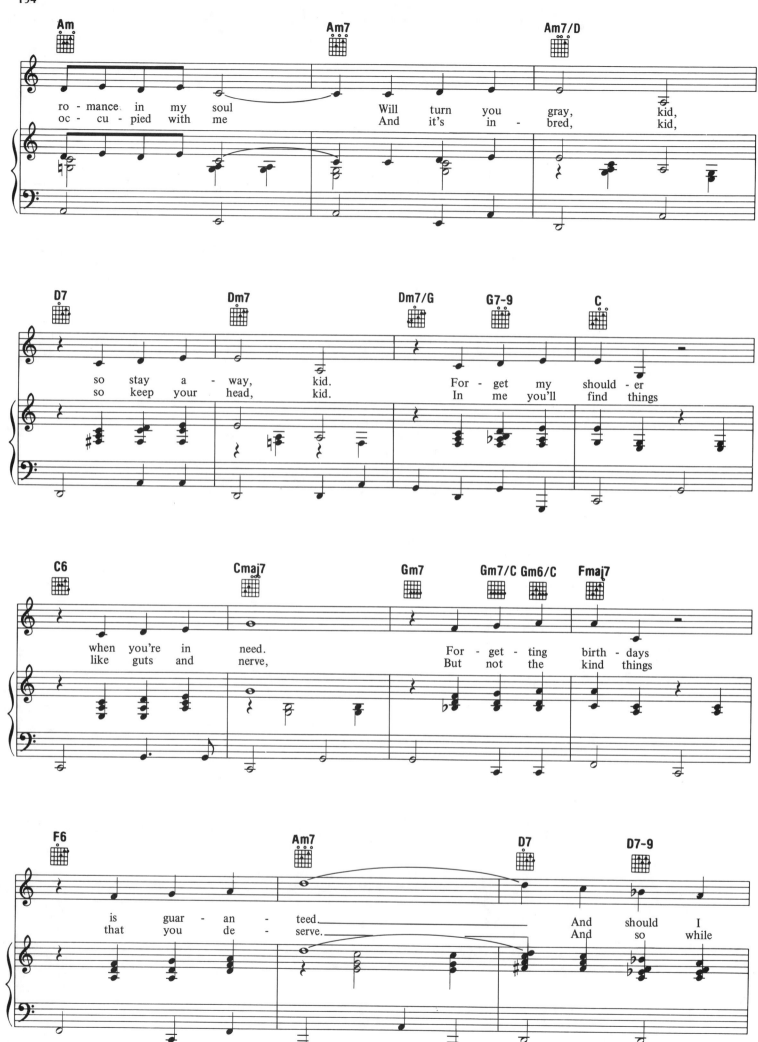

IF HE WALKED INTO MY LIFE

from MAME

Music and Lyric by
JERRY HERMAN

WE NEED A LITTLE CHRISTMAS

from MAME

Music and Lyric by
JERRY HERMAN

MAME
from MAME

Music and Lyric by
JERRY HERMAN

With a lilt

Chorus

1. You coax the blues right out of the horn, Mame,
2. You've brought the cake-walk back into style, Mame,

You charm the husk right off of the corn, Mame,
You make the weep-in' wil-low tree smile, Mame,

You've got the ban-joes strum-min' and plunk-in' out a tune to beat the
Your skin is Dix-ie sat-in, there's reb-el in your man-ner and your

BIG D
from THE MOST HAPPY FELLA

By FRANK LOESSER

JOEY, JOEY, JOEY
from THE MOST HAPPY FELLA

By FRANK LOESSER

STANDING ON THE CORNER
from THE MOST HAPPY FELLA

By FRANK LOESSER

Relaxed

HERMAN and BOYS:

Stand - ing on the cor - ner watch - ing all the girls go by,
Stand - ing on the cor - ner watch - ing all the girls go by,
Stand - ing on the cor - ner watch - ing all the girls go by,

Stand - ing on the cor - ner watch - ing all the girls go
Stand - ing on the cor - ner giv - ing all the girls the
Stand - ing on the cor - ner un - der - neath a spring - time

by Broth - er you don't know a nic - er oc - cu -
eye Broth - er if you've got a rich i - mag - i -
sky Broth - er you can't go to jail for what you're

THE IMPOSSIBLE DREAM
(THE QUEST)
from MAN OF LA MANCHA

Lyric by JOE DARION
Music by MITCH LEIGH

SHALOM
from MILK AND HONEY

Music and Lyric by
JERRY HERMAN

Moderate Waltz

Refrain

Dm   Dm(+7)   Dm7   Dm6   Dm(+5)   Dm

Sha - lom, Sha - lom, you'll find Sha - lom the nic - est greet - ing you

Em7   A7   Em7   A7   Gm6   A7

know; It means bon - jour, sa - lud, and skoal and

Em7   A7   Dmaj7   D6   G   Gmaj7

twice as much as hel - lo. It means a mil - lion

GOODNIGHT MY SOMEONE

from Meredith Willson's THE MUSIC MAN

Words and Music by
MEREDITH WILLSON

Slowly

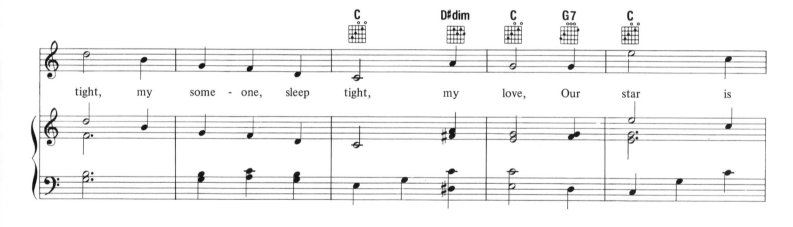

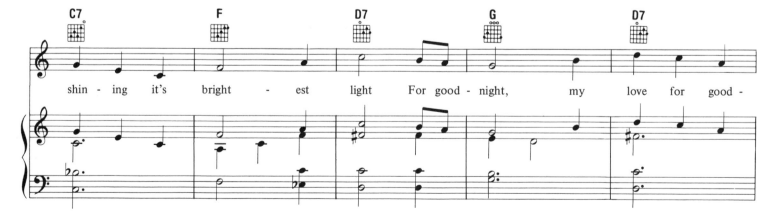

SEVENTY SIX TROMBONES

from Meredith Willson's THE MUSIC MAN

By MEREDITH WILLSON

TILL THERE WAS YOU

from Meredith Willson's THE MUSIC MAN

By MEREDITH WILLSON

LIDA ROSE
from Meredith Willson's THE MUSIC MAN

By MEREDITH WILLSON

ON THE STREET WHERE YOU LIVE
from MY FAIR LADY

Words by ALAN JAY LERNER
Music by FREDERICK LOEWE

I COULD HAVE DANCED ALL NIGHT
from MY FAIR LADY

Words by ALAN JAY LERNER
Music by FREDERICK LOEWE

THE RAIN IN SPAIN

from MY FAIR LADY

Words by ALAN JAY LERNER
Music by FREDERICK LOEWE

OKLAHOMA
from OKLAHOMA!

Lyrics by OSCAR HAMMERSTEIN II
Music by RICHARD RODGERS

PEOPLE WILL SAY WE'RE IN LOVE

from OKLAHOMA!

Lyrics by OSCAR HAMMERSTEIN II
Music by RICHARD RODGERS

I TALK TO THE TREES

from PAINT YOUR WAGON

Words by ALAN JAY LERNER
Music by FREDERICK LOEWE

BEWITCHED
from PAL JOEY

Words by LORENZ HART
Music by RICHARD RODGERS

He's a fool and don't I know it. But a fool can have his charms.
Love's the same old sad sen-sa-tion. Late-ly I've not have slept a wink

I'm in love and don't I show it, Like a babe in arms.
Since this half-pint im-i-ta-tion

Put me on the blink. I'm wild a-gain, Be-guiled a-gain, A

NEVER NEVER LAND
from PETER PAN

Lyric by BETTY COMDEN and ADOLPH GREEN
Music by JULE STYNE

Moderately

IF I RULED THE WORLD
from PICKWICK

Words by LESLIE BRICUSSE
Music by CYRIL ORNADEL

263

TELL ME ON A SUNDAY
from SONG & DANCE

Music by ANDREW LLOYD WEBBER
Lyrics by DON BLACK

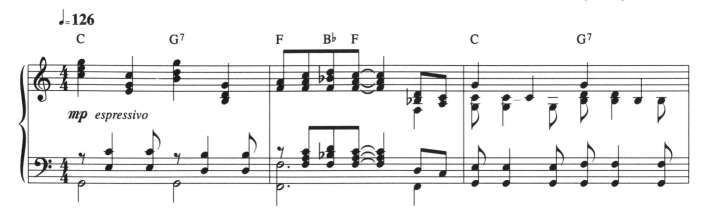

Don't write a let - ter when you want to leave,

don't call me at 3 a. m. from a friend's a - part - ment; I'd like to choose how I

EVERYBODY'S GOT A HOME BUT ME

from PIPE DREAM

Lyrics by OSCAR HAMMERSTEIN II
Music by RICHARD RODGERS

YESTERDAYS
from ROBERTA

Words by OTTO HARBACH
Music by JEROME KERN

FREEDOM
from SHENANDOAH

Lyric by PETER UDELL
Music by GARY GELD

Moderately

Free-dom ain't a state like Maine or Vir-gin-ia, Free-dom ain't a-cross some coun-ty line.
Free-dom ain't a beat that's leav-in' with-out ya, Free-dom ain't a place ya float to find.

Free-dom is a flame that burns with-in ya, Free-dom's in the state of mind.
Free-dom is the how ya think a-bout ya, Free-dom's in the state of mind.

(Finger snaps)

Free - dom, Free - dom, Free - dom, Free - dom.
Free - dom, Free - dom, Free - dom, Free - dom.

279

CAN'T HELP LOVIN' DAT MAN

from SHOW BOAT

Lyrics by OSCAR HAMMERSTEIN II
Music by JEROME KERN

MAKE BELIEVE
from SHOW BOAT

Lyrics by OSCAR HAMMERSTEIN II
Music by JEROME KERN

Lively

The game of ___ "just sup - pos - ing" ___ is the sweet - est ___ game I know. ___ Our ___ dreams are more ___ ro - man - tic than the world we see.

Cmaj7   C7

And if the things we dream a-bout don't hap-pen _ to be

F   Dm7♭5   C/G   Dm/G

so, _____ that's _ just an un-im-por-tant

G7   C   C#dim7

tech - ni - cal - i - ty. _____ We could

Slower
G7

make be - lieve _____ I love you, _____ on - ly

EDELWEISS
from THE SOUND OF MUSIC

Lyrics by OSCAR HAMMERSTEIN II
Music by RICHARD RODGERS

THE SOUND OF MUSIC
from THE SOUND OF MUSIC

Lyrics by OSCAR HAMMERSTEIN II
Music by RICHARD RODGERS

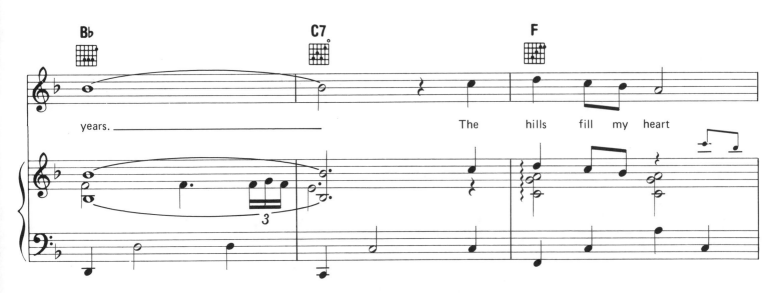

294

DO-RE-MI
from THE SOUND OF MUSIC

Lyrics by OSCAR HAMMERSTEIN II
Music by RICHARD RODGERS

HAPPY TALK
from SOUTH PACIFIC

Lyrics by OSCAR HAMMERSTEIN II
Music by RICHARD RODGERS

D.S. al Coda

CODA

true?_____ If you don't talk hap - py An' you nev - er have a

dream_____ Den you'll nev - er have a dream

come true!_____

SOME ENCHANTED EVENING

from SOUTH PACIFIC

Lyrics by OSCAR HAMMERSTEIN II
Music by RICHARD RODGERS

304

THIS NEARLY WAS MINE

from SOUTH PACIFIC

Lyrics by OSCAR HAMMERSTEIN II
Music by RICHARD RODGERS

THERE IS NOTHIN' LIKE A DAME
from SOUTH PACIFIC

Lyrics by OSCAR HAMMERSTEIN II
Music by RICHARD RODGERS

WITH ONE LOOK
from SUNSET BOULEVARD

Music by ANDREW LLOYD WEBBER
Lyrics by DON BLACK and CHRISTOPHER HAMPTON,
with contributions by AMY POWERS

NORMA: With one look I can break your heart, with one look I play ev-ery part.

I can make your sad heart sing. With one look you'll know all you need to know.

With one smile I'm the girl next door or the love that you've hun-gered for.

COME RAIN OR COME SHINE

from ST. LOUIS WOMAN

Words by JOHNNY MERCER
Music by HAROLD ARLEN

THEY'RE PLAYING MY SONG

from THEY'RE PLAYING OUR SONG

Words by CAROLE BAYER SAGER
Music by MARVIN HAMLISCH

8ba

HOW HIGH THE MOON

from TWO FOR THE SHOW

Words by NANCY HAMILTON
Music by MORGAN LEWIS

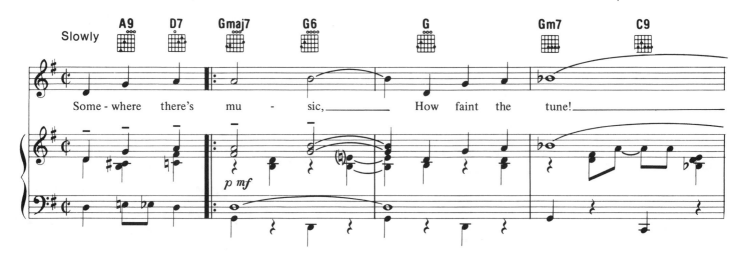

Some - where there's mu - sic,_____ How faint the tune!_____

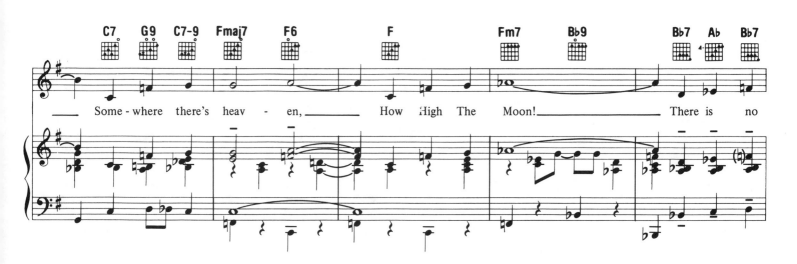

_____ Some - where there's heav - en,_____ How High The Moon!_____ There is no

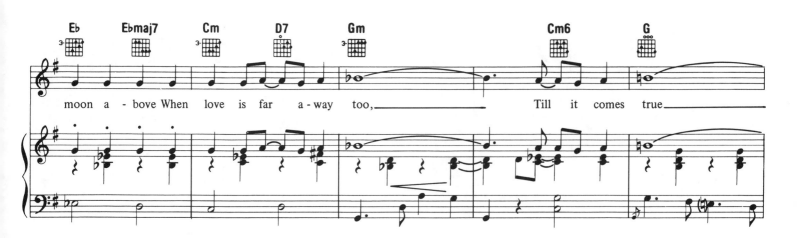

moon a - bove When love is far a - way too,_____ Till it comes true_____

I AIN'T DOWN YET

from THE UNSINKABLE MOLLY BROWN

Words and Music by
MEREDITH WILLSON

March tempo

I'm goan' to learn to read and write, I'm goan' to

see what there is to see, So if you go from

no-where on the road to some-where and you meet an-y-one you'll know it's

MY DARLING, MY DARLING

from WHERE'S CHARLEY?

By FRANK LOESSER

Moderately

THE NEW ASHMOLEAN MARCHING SOCIETY AND STUDENTS CONSERVATORY BAND

from WHERE'S CHARLEY?

By FRANK LOESSER

330

ONCE IN LOVE WITH AMY

from WHERE'S CHARLEY?

By FRANK LOESSER

Once in love with A - my,___ Al - ways in love with A - my,___ Ev - er and ev - er fas - cin - at - ed by 'er, Sets your heart a - fire___ to stay. Once you're kissed by

WHY DID I CHOOSE YOU?

from THE YEARLING

Lyric by HERBERT MARTIN
Music by MICHAEL LEONARD